MUSICAL

BIRDS

ARTWORK AND STORIES
BY
SHERRI LOUISE JONES

THE COMMUNICATION TREE COPYRIGHT © 2012

THE REALITY OF
EVERY DAY IS A MIRACLE

A long time ago I started writing stories about some of the things that I have noticed or came upon. I call it (The Reality of Every Day is a Miracle). This book has some of the short stories from that book. It also has some short stories from my book (Bird's Big and Small). If we look at all of the things that go on in one day, we can find many blessings.

THE COMMUNICATION TREE

MUSICAL BIRDS

Co-Authors

Brooklyn
Kast
&
Dennis
Dillard

Thank you
for your
songs!

A MIND OF INNOCENCE

Within a mind of innocence, a child is powerful enough to retain the memory of knowing love power and the reality of it. This is why it is important to remember the innocence of children and to teach them well. I very much appreciate being taught this as a child.

I have written these stories in deep respect to all. For the people who appreciate their love of being a part of this earth our mother and the tree of life, the grandchildren, the trees that grow and sprout roots, branches and leaves of love for generations to come. In hopes of a good future for all living things as we grow on our life's path on to other generations.

MUSICAL

BIRDS

CONTENTS

Songbird, 9

Flutes & Whistles, 15

Woodpecker, 16

Cat Movie, 18

Hey Little Blue Bird, 19

I Saw an Eagle, 26

Birds Love To Sing, 28

SONGBIRD

Within the Cherokee culture there is a bird called the songbird. It comes to people to tell a story and takes the peoples stories as a messenger. Many other birds are known as messengers. Pigeons were used in the past for carrying and delivering letters to people. Doves are known for carrying the message of love and peace. When I think of a dove I think of elegance and grace. When seeing a songbird I see perfect balance and grace.

A few days after thinking and writing some things about songbirds, I saw one of them on the television. It was very small and all black. It was dipping its whole body into ice cold water after food, then coming right back up. It amazed me that the tiny little bird was not frozen stiff. They must be pretty tough little birds. It was very well balanced and stayed in perfect balance while doing this. Its feet and legs stayed perched out of the water, while it whole body was bent forward and immersed under water, it didn't appear to be affected by the cold and got a piece of food. It went straight forward down then back up. It was unbelievably flexible, quick, accurate and not frozen. I was amazed with the accuracy and speed with pecking a tiny piece of food under water. The time being about one or two seconds from start to finish for each little piece of food.

Birds are able to go where they want to be. They are lucky with the ability to fly. Most tropical birds would not attempt to go in the ice cold water and would die quickly living in the cold. Tropical birds are brought here from another country. I was amazed as to that the little itty bitty songbirds heart and lungs did not give out. They stay in the environments where they have the ability to survive. I was not thinking at first. They are so tiny and that does not mean that they are not tough little birds. It is just nature and how this little bird is use to living. It obviously has the ability to live like that. They look very delicate and dainty. I noticed that all birds have different amazing strengths.

Many birds migrate during the winter to where it is not cold. They are seeking warmer weather and the preferred type of food. I see little birds at the water and birdbaths during the winter. They are usually just pecking at it to drink and bathe. I had never seen a little bird go under ice cold water like that before. It surprised and amazes meto see how quick, casual and *easy it was for the bird to do this. I started to think about it. Of course the feathers are waterproof. If the feathers are thick then the water would not affect the body. They must have thick skin. I know that many birds will die if they get into areas where the air does not circulate real well. They cannot breathe and they will suffocate. They have delicate hearts and lungs. This little bird had to have its mouth open while being under ice water to peck the food real quickly. It was not under water very long though. I am not a bird scientist, so it's a little bit of deep thought. The strangest little things amaze me.*

I have watched a little black and white black-capped chickadee, chickee that comes to eat at my bird feeder. The feeder is about a half of a foot from my doorway window. It's a nice closeup view and I love to see them that close. I went into the woods and was standing looking around and I heard a chirp nearby. I looked in the tree behind me and it was a little black and white chickee birdie. It seemed like it chirped at me. It flew off of the branch and I could not see where it went. Then I turned away and heard it again. I looked and it was on a different branch. I had the same feeling and am wondering if it was the same one that I had been feeding. I think that this one seemed to want my attention. It is a real tiny little bird. They have a real sweet little way about them.

There are many stories in the Cherokee culture about the little chickadees. The chickadee, tsigilili, chickee, is a songbird. They are known to represent truth within telling a story as to reminding a person to focus. They are known for being messengers of truth. I have been writing my stories and trying to make sure that I explain things in ways that people will understand them correctly. It was good timing for me with that little chickee. They are also associated with the number seven within many different cultures. The colors black and white mean balance to many cultures. They are very well balanced in the ways of constant movement. I noticed when the chickadee was at my feeder it did not land while it ate. It stayed in one spot in the air in perfect balance right above the feeder flapping its wings while it was eating what it had pecked. It stayed in my mind because I was recognizing the way it was balanced. I really liked it and see it in my mind as a nice little memory every so often since.

FLUTES & WHISTLES

The oldest flute documented was made of a vulture wing bone in Germany. It is believed to be over 35,000 years old. It is believed to be the oldest musical instrument found in history. Others were found in Germany believed to be 30,000 – 37,000 years old. They were from the wings of a swan and found in a cave. They have finger placement holes in them.

These were not the only types of birds that were used to make flutes on this earth. Some wing bones were also used as whistles. Many Native Americans use eagle bone whistles in particular ceremonies according to culture. These types of things were found in many different parts of the world. They are mostly highly spiritual within traditions and legends of origin. They are known to be very holy and for many different purposes of doctoring, summoning or making of music. Within the Native American cultures there is a purpose for every living thing. When things in nature pass away all parts have a use. So a use can be found for every part of an animal or bird.

WOODPECKER

It is said that the woodpecker is a drummer beating to its own drum with nature and mother earth with its own pattern and freedom. They wake people up to the truth and grounding for balance with the earth and clarity. Woodpeckers are in association spiritually with both the sun and moon.

The woodpecker was famous within many Native American tribes for pecking holes in a branch which made a flute. They are known for *bringing the flute to the many Native people. The flute has been used for many different reasons. One of the biggest purposes is to summon a loved one or for courtship. Some people like to create love songs with them.*

It is said that the spirit nature of the songs made from the flutes comes from the woods. When some people want to learn how to play one, they go to the woods alone to create and practice their own songs.

They have become very popular to many people around the world. Many people feel a very positive spiritual nature with playing and listening to them. They have many good spiritual purposes.

CAT MOVIE

I found an educational bird video with a picture of a cardinal on the cover. I was seeing a lot of cardinals around that time. I was interested in learning about them. When I played it my cats started watching it and became excited. My cat Star charged at the TV and stopped real fast in the prowl pounce position. The other cat Medicine got close to the screen and watched with excitement. Some flute music stared playing in one of the scenes. Medicine started lightly pawing the birds on the screen in sync with the music. It looked like a synchronized dance with her paws. Like a cat ballet dance or an orchestra conductor. She was very graceful. I didn't care for the movie but they loved it. Every once and a while I would yell, "Hey Medicine, I'm putting your movie in." She would run to the TV and wait with *excitement. She would watch it from the beginning to the end every time with no distractions. It's about a 30 minute show. It wasn't about just cardinals there were various birds.*

HEY LITTLE BLUE BIRD

I was talking to my friend Dennis on the telephone one day. I told him that I was writing books about my bird experiences. I had mentioned A little pretty bird that was blue. He said that he wrote a bird song for a CD then he sang it to me. He said that he was in Sedona, Arizona way high up on a hill praying and was visited by hundreds of little birds that were blue. He wrote a story and song about it. He writes and sings Native story songs for children. He said that this song was gifted to him by the spirit of those birds in Sedona. He mailed a CD of the song to me.

A few weeks after one of my sons came over with a little baby light blue parrot as a gift to me. I loved the parrot so my granddaughter and I started to sing Dennis's song to her. She was a smart little bird. The little bird watched me collect her feathers from the bottom of the cage and put them in clear bag.

One day I walked passed her and she made a loud noise. I turned around and she had a feather in her beak while looking at me, then she put her beak outside of the cage. I put my hand out and she placed the feather in my hand. She did the same thing the next day. She watched me make some earring out of them. She always seemed interested in watching me do things.

She was a whole lot of fun and real cute. She could find ways to escape and I was afraid that she would fly away. Wisconsin is not a good place for a tropical bird. She got outside one time and was hopping around the yard. I took her cage out and she got into it. I was glad that she didn't fly into the trees in the woods out here. She had a thing about the telephone speaker. She associated it with conversations and would start making very loud noises at certain people that I was talking too.

She also liked to be hand fed. She appreciated having food given to her.

Sometimes she would surprise me and make a tone or tunes that I had just done. She was still a baby and liked to practice her vocals. She could get pretty loud and feisty sometimes. What was funny is that she was not afraid of my dog or cat. She bit both of them right away. Neither the dog nor cat tried to hurt her at all. She realized that they liked her. Then they all became a cute little family of friends. They could walk around on the ground together and visit.

My granddaughter was six years old. She had just became attracted to Dennis's song and started singing it frequently. The bird was a parrot not a bluebird but a bird that was blue. The bluebird is a type of bird.

HEY LITTLE BLUE BIRD

Hey little blue bird in the sky
Why don't you come and just fly by
Hey little blue bird sitting in a tree
Why don't you come and sing a song for me.
Hey little blue bird don't you know
Singing and playing way to go
Hey little blue bird in the sky
Why don't you come and sit right by
Hey little blue bird don't you know
Come and share your spirit way to go
Hey little blue bird, hey little blue bird,
Hey little blue bird, hey little blue bird
Hey little blue bird in the sky

*Why don't you come and just say
hi
Hey little blue bird in the sky
Why don't you come and sit right
by
In the cedar and the sage
Singing the song to pass the day
Hey little blue bird, hey little blue
bird
Hey little blue bird, hey little blue
bird
Hey little blue bird, hey little blue
bird, hey little blue bird.*

By Dennis Dillard (White Bear)

I SAW AN EAGLE

My granddaughter Brooklyn and I were walking in the woods. A big golden eagle flew out of a tree. She made up a song about it. A few days later I was telling a neighbor lady about it. She is almost 90 years old. She said that around that same time a big golden eagle landed in the yard that we share. It was staring at her while facing her big picture window. It opened it wings and started flapping them while looking at her through the window. She spoke about this with excitement. We had wondered if it was the same eagle and if that was where it went. Brooklyn sang the song to her.

She is one of the nicest and friendliest elder women I have ever met. Many children in the neighborhood enjoy her kindness. When she sees them, she always smiles and tells them *what good kids they are. She has a way about her that just sparkles when she speaks. I believe that the eagle was a message from the creator letting her know that she is blessed. Eagles and hawks like to make whistling sounds. We hear the hawks outside whistling almost every day.*

I SAW AN EAGLE

I saw an eagle flying from a tree.
I saw an eagle flying to the east.
I came with grandma
and a dog named Honey Bun.
We went up the hill
and down the hill again.
We searched everywhere for it
and it was gone.
My grandma and I put tobacco out.

By: Brooklyn Barbra Kast,
Created 4/1/11

BIRDS LOVE TO SING

Birds love to sing, each one has its own individual sounds and tones of a chirp, tweet or whistle. Some birds sing love songs to each other.

Some tropical birds like to sing and make tones in our human languages. Birds from all around the world like to sing and make many different kinds of musical sounds. They are in tune with nature. If a person sings real pretty another might say. It was sung like a bird.

A person should never be afraid to sing. Singing is good for the mind, body and spirit. We all sound different and are not all the same. We are individual and all have our own different ways of expression.

Many songs have tones and tunes that are healing. Many people sing prayer songs to (God) the creator or because it makes them feel good. Singing makes people feel happy and good. Our singing voices are beautiful and are not all the same. What some think is beautiful some might not, then others might. It does not matter as long as it makes us feel good. Not everybody likes or has the exact same sounds. The birds never seem to worry about what others think or even if they listen. They just express themselves. Sing to your own natures tunes.

Some people take music lessons so that they can learn about many different tones, we are all born with our own natural tones. To sing whatever we like is part of our freedom. So just be free and sing like a bird. It is all good!

Children need to learn how to care for one another and the earth. We need to teach them about humanity, kindness and gentleness within their own nature. One of the main things to learn is that we are all equal within creation, discrimination is a sin.

They need to know how to care for the birds, animal and the earth. The future is upon them. We need to teach it as a responsibility with love and respect.

CHIRP CHIRP!

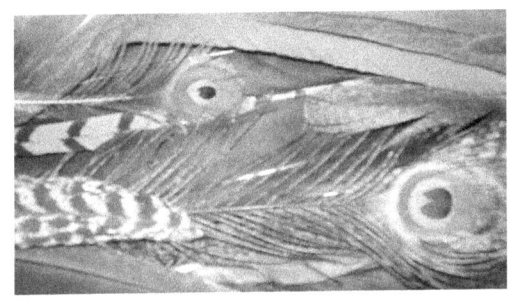

Understanding cultrual
differences is knowing
that we are all
One.

About The Author

I am an Interfaith Minister, a preacher of equal rights. I am culturally mixed by heritage (Irish, Native American, English, Scottish, Spanish, French and?) My Father's Mother was Native American and most of my beliefs are Native. I believe in freedom of speech and freedom of religious rights, freedom from all forms of discrimination (race, religion, culture, disability, diversity, age and gender.) We are all one on this earth our mother and we are all created equal.

May the Creator Bless You!

Sherri Louise Jones

Chirp!

~

THE END